Wh ave

to go to bed?

FOX EYE
PUBLISHING

Why do I have to go to bed now?

Because you need to give
your body and mind
a rest.

Why do I need to give my body a rest?

Because you have been busy today.

Parts of your body will be a bit worn out and it needs time to repair itself.

Why do I need to give my mind a rest?

Because you have experienced
a lot of new things today.

Your brain needs to pause
so it can sort and store away
these new thoughts
as memories.

Why do I need these memories?

Because that is how we learn. We remember what was nice to touch ...

... and what
hurt us.

What was
good ...

... and what
was bad.

But Why
can you stay up later than me?

Because, you have
so much more learning and
growing and dreaming
to do than me.

Goodnight. Sweet dreams little
one.

Let's find out about sleep.

Turn the page over to discover the answers to these questions.

What would happen if I didn't sleep for one day?
What would happen if I didn't sleep for 3 days?
Why do some grown ups snore?

Let's find out about sleep.

The answers are...

One third of our lives we spend sleeping.

Dreaming is how our minds sort important memories from unimportant ones.

You would do everything slower, and become grumpy.
You'd be ill, and start seeing things that were not there.
When they breathe it makes floppy parts of their throats rattle about. This makes the snoring sound.

How to use this book

You can read this book with one child or a group of children.

The book can be used to begin a discussion around complex questions such as learning why we have to go to bed.

The book is also a reading aid, with enlarged and repeated words to help children to develop their reading skills.

How to read the story

Before beginning the story, ensure that the children you are reading to are relaxed and focused.

Take time to look at the enlarged words and the illustrations, and discuss what this book might be about before reading the story.

New words can be tricky for young children to approach.

Sounding them out first, slowly and repeatedly, can help children to learn the words and become familiar with them.

Did you spot
the Tardigrade
hiding in
this book?

First published in 2023 by Fox Eye Publishing
Unit 31, Vulcan House Business Centre,
Vulcan Road, Leicester, LE5 3EF
www.foxeyepublishing.com

Written and illustrated by Simon Couchman

ISBN 978-1-80445-349-0

A catalogue record for this book is available from the British Library.

Printed in China

Titles in the Series

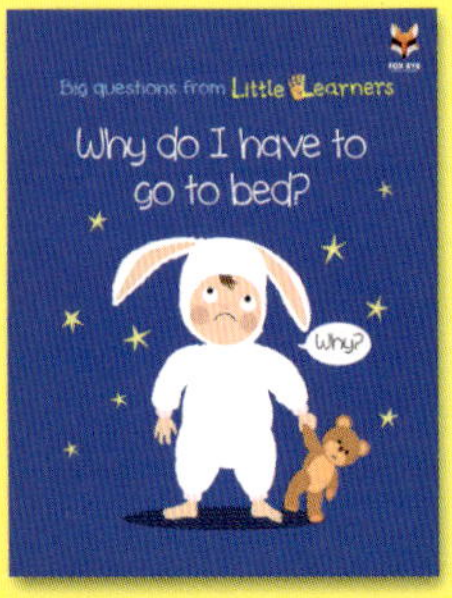

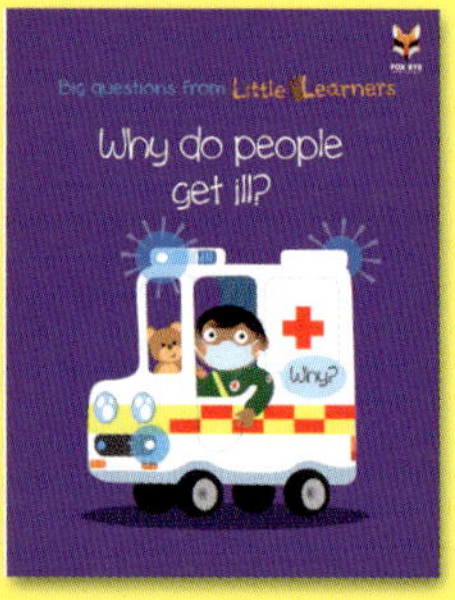

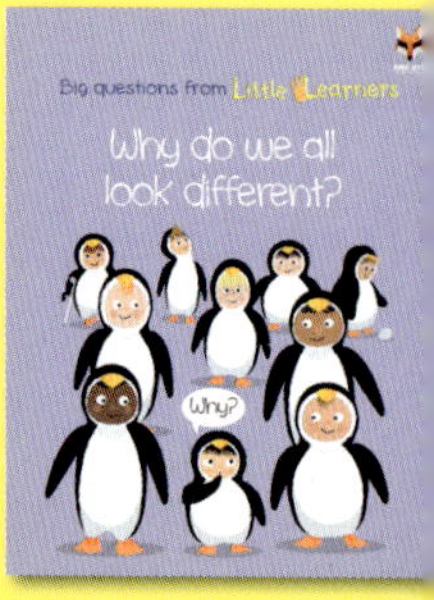

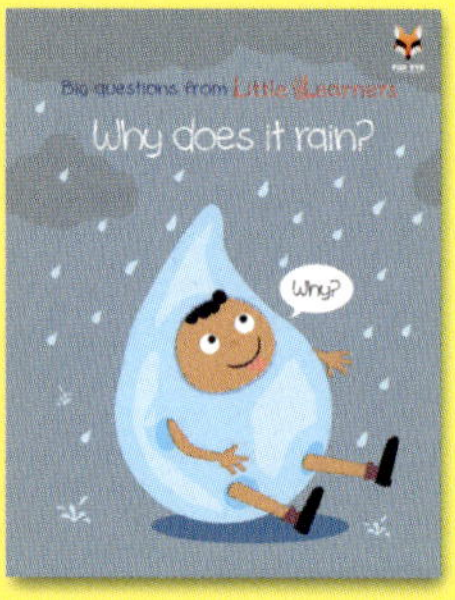

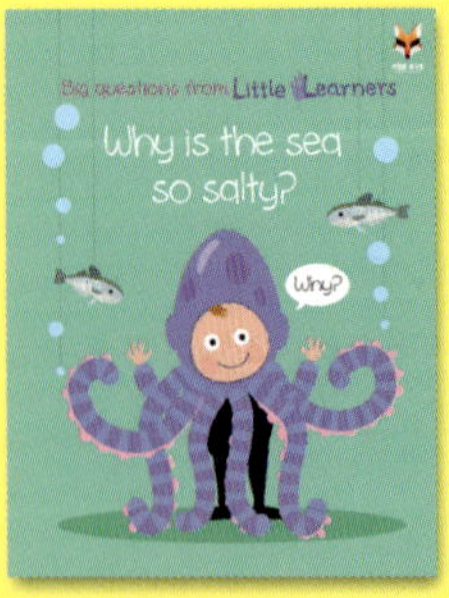

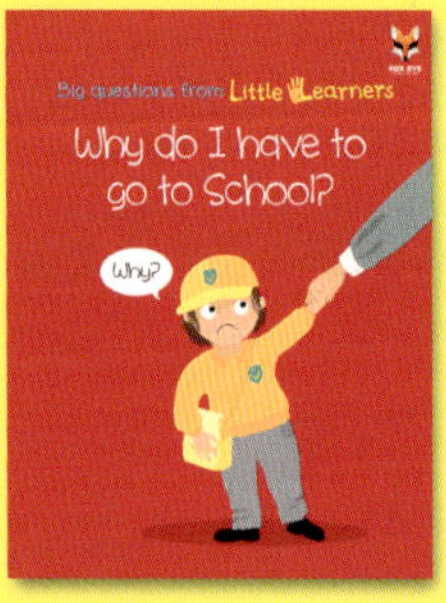